I made this book for the kids who get teased. You are very special. You are great the way you are.
Be happy and be safe. I believe in you!

~ Sofia Moses

When you do your best, you are doing a great job.

Kids, keep working at what is hard for you and keep trying to make your dreams come true.
Don't listen to kids who say you can't do something.
I know you can do it! I believe in you!

~ Monica Moses

<u>I dedicate this book to all children, in particular those with special needs:</u>
I want you to know -
You do not deserve to be bullied. It is not your fault.
You are valuable.
You are important.
You deserve to have friends and to be loved.
You deserve to be celebrated for who you are!
You deserve good things and happiness.
You CAN make your dreams to come true ~
I believe in you!

~ Susanna Moses

No part of this publication may be reproduced, stored in a retrieval system or transmitted in any form or by any means, electronic, mechanical, photocopying, recording, or otherwise, without written permission of the publisher. For information regarding permission, write to Moses Publishing Company, Inc. PO Box 120833, New Brighton, MN 55112.

ISBN 978-0996024693

Copyright © 2013 by Susanna Moses, Monica Moses and Sofia Moses. All rights reserved. Published by Moses Publishing Company, Inc. PO Box 120833, New Brighton, MN 55112. All associated drawings and logos are trademarks or registered trademarks of Susanna Moses, Monica Moses and Moses Publishing Company, Inc. Printed in the U.S.A.

Nectar

The Unique Bumble Bee

Written by Susanna & Sofia Moses ~ Illustrated by Monica Moses ~ Colorist Sofia Moses

Hi. My name is Nectar. I am in kindergarten.
I am a bumble bee. I am unique.
I was born without a stinger.
That makes me fly a little crooked, but I am fast.

I have many friends. They are unique too.
We all look different on the outside, but we have the same feelings on the inside. We like a lot of the same things. We always have fun together.

I sound different than most bees. The other bees wings make the sound, buzz buzz buzz.
My wings sound like, bizz bizz bizz.

Some bugs make fun of me. That makes me feel sad.

My friend Fuego the Dragonfly has one wing smaller than the other. He cannot fly yet.
He practices everyday. He does not give up.

Sometimes other bugs tease him too.
They say mean things that hurt his feelings.
That makes him feel angry and sad.

My friend Wiggles the spider cannot spin a web yet.
She works on web-making everyday.
Sometimes she feels frustrated that she cannot spin because she tries so hard.

She gets teased too. The older spiders cruelly sing, "Who ever heard of a spider who can't spin a web?" I do not like it when others tease us, make fun of us or call us cruel names.

Teasing is not nice.
If you tease someone it will hurt their feelings.
Making fun of others is not nice either.
If you make fun of others, they will feel sad.
And it is never okay to call others cruel names.

Flutter the butterfly is our friend.
She is nice to us. When we feel sad she says,
"You can do it! Keep trying! I believe in you!"
This makes us feel better and work harder.

Our friend Dot the ladybug cheers us on, too.
She shouts, "Good Job. You are doing great!"
That makes us feel happy and proud of our work.

It is good to use happy words.
Words that show others that you care about them.
When you are nice and encourage others,
they will want to be your friend.

I am thankful for all of my friends.
My mommy says love means to be nice to each other.
I love my friends and I know they love me.
We always help each other, especially when something is hard for one of us to do.

We work together and help each other.
We try hard and do our best.
We are proud of each other.
We are proud of ourselves.

Nectar and his friends continued practicing when suddenly Nectar shouted,
"Oh no, look! The big bugs are stealing my honey pods!"
The bugs snickered as they flew away.

SPLAT! The bugs hit a leaf. The honey squirted everywhere gluing them to it.
SQUIRM. SQUIRM. "Help! We can not get loose!"
SPLOOSH! SPLASH!
They hit the water as it rushed toward the falls.

"**HELP US! HELP US!**" they shrieked.
Nectar and his friends flew swiftly toward the stuck bugs.
Thinking quickly, Wiggles said, "Nectar, grab my thread."
Then Fuego flew her across to the other side.
"Grab on and we will pull you to shore," yelled Nectar.

Nectar, Wiggles and Fuego rescued the bugs who had been so cruel to them.
The big bee and his friends felt bad for what they had done. He said, "Thank you for saving us. We are sorry we teased you and took your honey. You bugs are pretty cool."

"You are welcome," answered Nectar, "We forgive you.
Would you bugs like to BEE our friends?"
The big bugs smiled and said,
"Yes. And we will **Bee Nice** from now on."

Is there something you cannot do that
other kids can?
What *can* you do that makes you feel proud of yourself?
Does anyone make fun of you, tease you
or call you cruel names?

How do you feel when that happens?
Do you stand up for others if someone is cruel to them?
What happy words can you say to others that will make them feel good about themselves?

Making fun of, teasing and calling others cruel names is called <u>bullying</u>. Bullying is NOT nice. Bullying hurts. If someone makes fun of you, teases you, calls you a cruel name or you see this happening to someone else, tell them to stop. If they do not stop, tell a grown up.

BEE NICE CLUB

I PROMISE

TO ALWAYS

BEE NICE

Be kind, share, help others, and be a good friend

Nectar asked the big bugs if they all wanted to be in the **BEE NICE CLUB**.
There is only one rule – **Bee Nice.** This means to choose to be kind, to share, to help others, to be a good friend. Would *you* like to choose to be kind and be a member of the **Bee Nice Club?**

Raise your hand and say what Nectar says,
"I promise to **Bee Nice** ~
to be kind, to share, to help others,
and to be a good friend"

_____
is in the

BEE NICE CLUB

This is a badge to photocopy and give to the children.
Have them fill in their name, color in and cut it out.

You do not have to try to be like anyone else.

You are perfect just the way you are.

You are unique.

That means there is no one else like you.

Nectar says,

"Always do your best and just BEE you!

BEE nice to others even if they are different from you.

Everyone has a purpose.

Everyone likes to have friends!"

_____

is an official member of the

BEE NICE CLUB

I promise to BEE NICE,
Be kind, share, help others and be a good friend.

Photocopy this page. Give one to each child.
Have them fill in their name, color in, cut out
and keep.

Sofia's original drawing of Nectar when she was 4 1/2 years old.

Sofia is creative and has a vibrant imagination. She is involved in musical theatre, loves to act, design and don costumes, sing and dance. Sofia is also into fashion, helping others and everything else a rambunctious five year-old enjoys!

Sofia, now 6, created Nectar a few months after her fourth birthday. Walking home from the park one day she said, "Mommy, I want to write a story about a bumble bee. I would call him Nectar ."

I asked her what the story would be about and she told me it would be about a little bee in kindergarten who was different than the other bees. She wanted to tell kids her own age that being cruel is not nice. She had witnessed teasing of her big sister, Monica, who has autism. She did *not* like seeing her sister being made fun of. Sofia told me details about the story, Nectar's friends, the "bad bugs", where they all lived and the story blossomed from there.

Sofia and Monica helped write the story and gave me the final approval. Sofia drew the first rendition of Nectar and Monica used that drawing to create the characters. The finished product is interactive and can easily be used as an enhancement for anti-bullying campaigns. It promotes responsibility and respect by offering a young audience the opportunity to make the choice to "**BEE NICE**" to others. This story reinforces working hard, pride in a job well done and believing in oneself no matter what others may say. I have included discussion questions to engage the listeners in open dialog about different abilities and bullying. Also included is a ribbon and an official member of the **BEE NICE CLUB** certificate for the children to decorate, sign and keep. My goal is that Nectar's image and story will deeply influence children, from a young age, to be respectful of other people's feelings and learn to not simply accept differences, but to see diversity as a positive thing. Everyone can be a friend to others if they choose to!

Other Nectar Titles to come:

Nectar Learns to Share
Nectar Learns How to Stay Safe

Please log onto
www.mosespublishing.com
for information on other Sofia books.

Monica, Sofia's big sister, is a self taught artist. After a rapid and extensive developmental and motor ability regression, she was diagnosed with severe autism at the age of three. Monica has worked extremely hard to be where she is today. Overcoming the effects of Autism in her life, has been difficult, but Monica's resolve and fearlessness always makes her forge ahead. According to her, anything is possible.

Her remarkable recovery has inspired other families who have children with autism and related neurological disorders. Monica now desires to help other children who have "lost their words and have a hard time doing things."

You can read more about her incredible story and our family's journey with autism in the book, *Monica's Silent World*, available at www.mosespublishing.com.

I am so proud to be the mother of Monica and Sofia'. I have truly been blessed beyond measure to have such loving, beautiful, intelligent and talented children. We desire to help others with every work we co-create.

A little bit about me; I have worked with children with varying exceptionalities for over 20 years. I have been involved in training, advocacy and raising awareness of Autism, through the non-profit I established in 2001, Hand in Hand Autism Resources, Inc. I created and hosted a television special about Autism, which transitioned into a world wide radio program, in English and Spanish, on Autism One Radio for a season. I took a break from the radio due to some health issues with Monica, later diagnosed as diabetes. During my hiatus, Sofia was born. I will be resuming a video series, but on my YouTube channel. I *am* fluent in Spanish. I write poetry, non-fiction, children's stories, inspirational works, music, scripts, I am a vocalist, public speaker, a Chaplain and an ordained minister.

I hope that the Nectar series and Monica's Silent World series, based on my life raising Monica and illustrated by her, will inspire others and promote understanding and acceptance of these amazing people who have Autism. I pray Monica's recovery and success as an illustrator and in her artistic career will further encourage other talented individuals with special needs to pursue their dreams.

For more information about the Moses family, please log on to;

www.susannamoses.com   www.handinhand4autism.org   www.monicassilentworld.com
www.joanmoses.com   www.mosespublishing.com   www.cartooncool.org